What others are saying about The Nigerian Dream.

Accurate documentation of memories is very important otherwise it is politicized and used against the people through gaslighting. What Dr Mo has done, is to ensure we never forget the true state of things as they occurred and also proffer a way forward in the midst of all the chaos. He has done this while in the trenches to ensure that the threat to our democracy is eliminated through the legally accepted manner. Dr Mo has shown his commitment to a nation that works for all.

- Aisha Yesufu
Nigerian activist and businesswoman. Co-founded the #BringBackOurGirls Movement.

The Nigerian Dream by Dr Moses Paul aka Madmo is masterfully written with metaphors and stories that are factually and emotionally resonant. It also presents a powerful message of hope and a call to action.

- Dr. David Ogula
Human Capital Management Consultant. Former VP and Dean School of Business and Management Studies, Apollo, University, Great Fall, Montana, USA.

Dr Mo is an unapologetic Nigerian who is fighting for a new Nigeria. This book says a great deal about his passion in his genuine quest to get the populace to think outside the box. It challenges the current state of affairs taking us back to the past while standing on the present and projecting into the future the new Nigeria that is possible. A masterpiece in my opinion.

- Ndidi Mbagwu -Mental Health Practitioner in NHS United Kingdom. MSc Mental Health Interventions.

The Nigeria Dream.
To reflect is to dream. But the dream of a patriot has heart and Soul.

It is not the best kept secret in the world that Dr Moses Paul is a thoroughbred Nigerian patriot. In this volume, Dr. Mo dares to dream the Patriots' dream. It is an admixture of hope, frustration and stubborn positive affirmation as he reflects on 63 years of struggle for nation building in Nigeria.

In offering synopsis short histories of other countries' experience he uses them to project the possibilities if Governance would do right by Nigerians.

The motivational pitch swells from Cry the beloved country lamentation and rises to a YES WE CAN admonition. Encouraging. The only trouble is that aspirational texts are not enough. People have to be prepared to leave their comfort zones and do something. Sacrifice and risks may go with standing up to do something but it brings results. Thankfully Mo himself is living proof of commitment to do something.

- Patrick O Utomi (Prof)
Professor of political economy and management expert. He is a Fellow of the Institute of Management Consultants of Nigeria and a former presidential candidate. Founder, Centre for Value in Leadership and the African Democratic Congress.

The "Nigeria Dream" by Dr Mo is about familiar issues that plague Nigeria, it goes into details of the causes and effects, and juxtaposes Nigeria in a comparative context showing how she has not measured up.

The book however, holds unto the dream of Nigeria's potential for greatness and challenges individual Nigerians to arise and confront the fault-lines of their history and push aside the barriers to Nigeria's emergence as a country of outstanding promise.

The text is laced with statistics and accounts of the developmental journeys of other countries as well as the inspiration behind their success stories. How they were able to break through and surmount unimaginable odds to achieve progress particularly through human advancement. The book embeds the SDGs in its logic of recounting the new found fortunes of emerging nations. Their progress demonstrates how the pursuit of these goals, provides a matrix for judging their transformation in relation to others and in global terms.

Overall, the book deploys a conversational style to draw its reader attention and gain his or her focus in what the dream for

Nigeria and its peoples is all about. In the end, it leaves many unstated nations for our imagination and captivation to dwell on.

Amb. Nkoyo Toyo
Lawyer, development activist, and politician. She served as a member of the Nigerian House of Representatives, and as ambassador to Ethiopia and Djibouti and Permanent Representative to the African Union.

Madmo has a spirit of faith and dodgenesss driven by his love for everyday people, Nigeria and Africa. He writes and speaks out of Objective clarity, decisiveness and fearlessness. The "Nigerian Dream" by Dr Moses Paul is our reality past, present and future.

Comrade Deji Adeyunju
Lawyer and Human Rights Activist.
Chairman, Centre For Liberty and Convener Concerned Nigerians.

Dr Mo is a tireless servant uplifting Nigeria. I recommend "The Nigerian Dream" for all Nigerians home and abroad.

- Dr. Nell Diallo
A bilingual professional serving as Executive Director of International and Corporate Relations at MedShare,
Atlanta, USA.

DR MOSES PAUL

The NIGERIAN Dream

A NEW NIGERIA IS POSSIBLE

This book is available from the National Library of Nigeria

ISBN: **978-978-799-238-8**

Printed and bound in Nigeria

PETER PIPER
PROMOTIONS PUBLICATION
Road A1, Pentville Estate, Lokogoma
Abuja, Nigeria+ 234 803 319 4072

To every citizen who is committed to the vision of a united and just Nigeria. Who is working tirelessly to achieve this vision for all Nigerians, regardless of their background or beliefs.

To the leadership that is committed to upholding the values of merit, representation, rule of law, equity, accountability, fairness, justice, responsibility, and a focus on the future of Nigeria.

May this book inspire all Nigerians to work towards a better future for their country.

FORWORD

In the realm of Nigeria's transformation, I discern a remarkable shift. As a new generation of Nigerians come into their own, propelling the nation towards a future of immense potential, Nigeria finds itself at a pivotal juncture, undergoing a profound evolution that encompasses not only politics and governance but also leadership and all other condiments of society. This momentous period is replete with significant shifts that are reshaping our collective approach and challenging the long-standing paradigms of the old order.

The emergence of a new Nigeria hangs delicately in the balance between the agents of change and the tenacious grip of the established political order. The tussle between these opposing forces embodies the struggle for the nation's destiny, as the winds of transformation buffet against the entrenched currents of tradition and resistance. Yet, amidst this intricate dance, the inevitability of a new Nigeria, shimmering on the horizon, cannot be denied.

To reflect is to dream. But the dream of a patriot has heart and soul. It is not the best kept secret in the world that Dr. Moses Paul is a thoroughbred Nigerian patriot. In this volume, Dr. Mo dares to dream the Patriots' dream. It is an admixture of hope, frustration and stubborn positive affirmation as he reflects on 63 years of struggle for nation building in Nigeria. In offering synopsis on short histories of other countries' experience, he projects the beam of possibilities if Government would do right by Nigerians. The motivational pitch swells from Cry the Beloved Country lamentation and rises to a 'Yes We Can!' admonition. Encouraging.

The Nigerian dream, both tangible and elusive, presents itself as a reflection of our current reality-a reflection that illuminates the contours of our challenges while simultaneously showcasing the immense possibilities that lie within our grasp. The dream beckons us to contemplate our role in shaping the destiny of our nation and compels us to ponder a critical question: Will we, as a collective, convert this dream into a tangible reality, one that uplifts and inspires, or will we, by our inaction or missteps, allow it to morph into a haunting nightmare?

Indeed, the stakes are high, for the Nigerian dream holds the key to our personal aspirations and the shared fate of our nation. It encapsulates the hopes, aspirations, and yearnings of every Nigerian, resonating deeply within the hearts of individuals from diverse backgrounds and walks of life. Our future prosperity, unity, and progress are intricately woven to our ability to harness the immense potential that this dream embodies.

Aspirational texts are not enough. People have to be prepared to leave their comfort zones and do something. Sacrifice and risks may go with standing up to do something but it brings results. Thankfully, Dr. Mo is living proof of commitment to do something. It is incumbent upon us, as citizens of this great nation, to navigate the crossroads of history with sagacity and foresight. We must actively partake in the remaking of

Nigeria, endeavoring to surmount the challenges that lie in our path. By embracing the dream, we embrace a collective responsibility to bring about positive change, transforming Nigeria into a beacon of progress, justice, and prosperity for all its citizens.

The road ahead may be arduous, fraught with obstacles and complexities, but within this very struggle lies the promise of a brighter tomorrow. Let us seize this opportune moment to shape a new Nigeria, one that embodies the values of inclusivity, equity, and social harmony. By doing so, we will not only honor the sacrifices of our forebears but also secure a legacy of hope and promise for generations to come.

- **Pat Utomi (Prof).**

CONTENTS

CHAPTER I

The Men Of Sixty-Three

Kena had always been a dreamer, with dreams and hopes for a better future that would soon be his. But he was the type of man who never seemed to find fulfillment or, in fact, the courage to change his situation.

He would complain to his friends and family about never getting ahead, but he did nothing to achieve his goals. His fear of failure, and his comfort with the status quo, kept him from taking risks or making significant changes in his life.

Kena remained trapped in a cycle of discontent and unfulfillment, unable to break free from his own self-imposed restrictions and limitations. He became increasingly bitter as the years passed, trapped in a never-ending cycle of an unsatisfying life.

While Kena's inability to do anything about his situation was the crux of his problem, his complaint was not unique, as many people feel trapped in a mundane routine and struggle to break free from it.

In contrast, our dear Kena has failed where others have succeeded.

And it was due to his refusal to understand that doing nothing is far worse than taking action, even if it means making mistakes in the process, that he failed.

It is better to try and fail than never to try at all. Kena was familiar with this concept. This notion, he insisted, was the foundation of his life. He often shared this notion with others, hoping to inspire them to live with the same mindset.

Kena attempted to demonstrate his adherence to that philosophy at various points throughout his life. He tried to climb the **Sankwala Mountains** at the age of 20 but returned due to "severe altitude sickness," and later tried again at the age of 25 but was unable to because he feared terrible weather conditions.

When Kena turned 30, he decided he was ready to quit his job and start his own business, but he concluded that 35 was a better age to start. Despite spending the next five years gaining valuable experience and laying the groundwork for his future business, he felt restless and abandoned his entrepreneurial dreams.

But as the years passed, Kena became more disillusioned with his life, and he started to feel as though he was going through the motions rather than truly living.

He'd frequently catch himself thinking about the life he could have had if he had only been brave enough to take the risks required to achieve his goals.

Kena then decided to take up a hobby in his mid-forties. He reasoned that immersing himself in something creative might bring him happiness. He dabbled in photography, drawing, cooking, and gardening. However, nothing seemed to stick, and his joy was fleeting.

He gave up every hobby with an excuse. *When everyone has smartphones, photography seems like such a waste of time. There is no use in drawing without any artistic ability. That is the equivalent of attempting to pilot a plane without knowing how to, which was a bad idea. Cooking was only a pastime if you liked the smell of burnt food. And gardening was incredibly hard for a man his age.*

DON'T LET THE FEAR OF UNCERTAINTY PREVENT YOU FROM MAKING A CHANGE.

Finally, he decided to focus on himself and signed up for a gym membership. He reasoned that if he invested in his body and health, he could, at least, improve that aspect of his life. However, after his second visit to the gym, he realized that it was not enough to make him happy. Kena got frustrated and was unsure of what to do next.

After never fully committing to anything at all, Kena turned 63. He felt the best part of his life was behind him, and there was no reason to try anymore. *What else could one do? He couldn't possibly start something new and find something meaningful.* He decided to quit pursuing his passion.

***

Then, there's Abeba, a man with a lifetime of experience and wisdom. Wisdom he'd gained through decades of struggle and striving; and a bittersweet sense of unfulfillment.

He had witnessed the world change in ways he never imagined possible, but he still felt like something was missing from his life—a sense of purpose that had eluded him for years.

He'd seen a lot in his nearly 63 years. He'd climbed

mountains, swam in oceans, witnessed wars fought and forgotten, made and lost friends, and lived life to the fullest for as long as he could. But he had also felt the deep loneliness of the end of a period of his life, a loneliness he couldn't escape no matter how hard he tried to fill his time.

Abeba always wanted to find his place in life. Ever since he was a young man, he had felt a gnawing in his heart—an unspoken sense that he needed to do something great, something meaningful. But despite his best attempts, he had never quite been able to work out what it was.

As he aged, as all humans do, the feeling only grew more intense. After his 62nd birthday, it had become a constant presence in his mind, something he was desperate to solve. He felt a pressing need to find answers before it was too late.

So when his daughter, who lived on the other side of the country, called one day and asked if he could come and stay with her for a while, Abeba saw it as a sign from the universe.

Maybe he needed to step away from his life to allow himself time to think and finally figure out the answer to his lifelong question.

EMBRACE THE UNKNOWN, AND TRUST THAT YOU CAN ADAPT AND THRIVE

A NEW NIGERIA IS POSSIBEE

They arranged for him to stay at her house for a month. He packed his belongings and traveled to her home. As soon as he arrived, Abeba knew he'd made the right choice. He felt a sense of peace, calm, and belonging that he had never experienced before.

On the second day of his stay, he walked around the neighborhood. He marveled at how beautiful the world was, how brightly the sun shone, and how the birds sang. That was when he realized what his "something great" was.

Back at his daughter's house, he mapped out a plan. He intended to build a community for the elderly who didn't have anywhere else to go—a place with love, warmth, and a sense of belonging.

After a month, he had a detailed plan for making it happen. He saw no reason to wait and took immediate action by contacting the appropriate people to assist in making his vision a reality.

Abeba found his purpose at the age of 63. He discovered his calling in life and set out to make a difference. It was finally time to live up to his potential. With a clear sense of purpose, he worked tirelessly towards his goals.

It had taken him a lifetime to achieve inner peace. He'd learned to maneuver around his sorrow, discomfort, and sometimes wounds.

But he'd done it, and he finally felt fulfillment. Abeba felt a deep contentment and a sense of satisfaction because, ultimately, he had achieved something great and important. He had put in a lot of hard work and dedication toward his goal, and now it had paid off.

That was enough to fill a man with contentment, and Abeba felt it. He was content with his aging body, pleased with his home of peace, content with the relationships that had stood the test of time, and found satisfaction even in his solitude.

He had done something great despite his advanced age and the adversity and hardship that came with it. Abeba accomplished something remarkable and changed his world at the age of 63.

He was inspiring, demonstrating that age is not a barrier to greatness and that dreams, regardless of age, can come true. Abeba was living proof that the number 63 could be 10, 20, or 36.

Real change can occur anytime; all you have to do is reach out and take action.

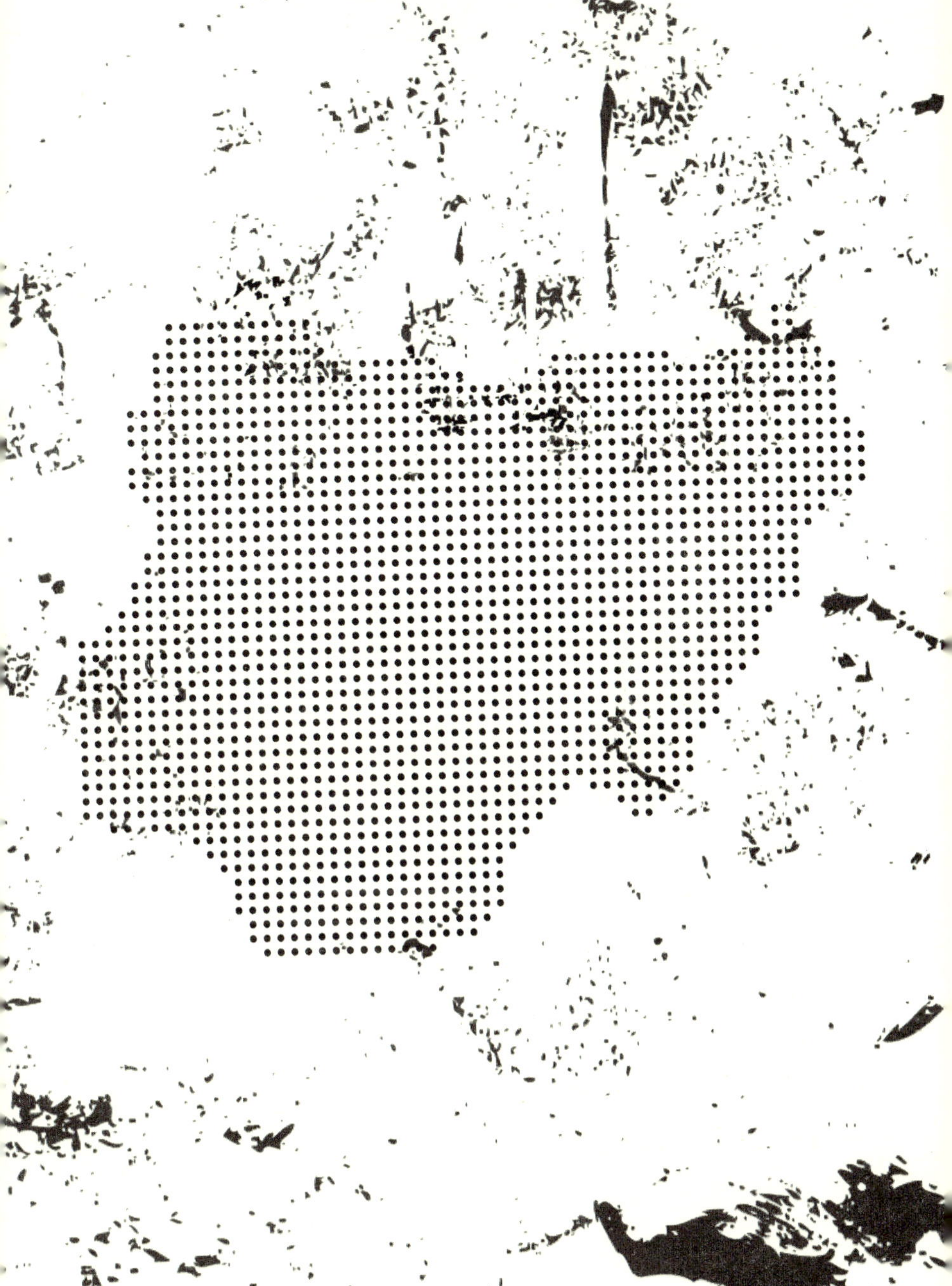

Chapter 2

Our Once Beloved Mother

Rain continues to fall, and the children of this land are freezing. We seek comfort in the arms of a cruel mother who is unloving and unforgiving and truly despises her children. But it wasn't always this way.

Oh no! This mother was once so loving, caring, and attentive to the needs of her children. Regrettably, she now seems distant and uninterested in their lives.

And I understand; our once-caring mother is about to turn 63. Her bones are tired, and her energy levels have plummeted. What's more, the men who had sworn love to her and made vows to her appear to have forgotten the meaning of those words.

They, too, have grown distant, leaving her lonely and

unloved. It breaks my heart to see her in this condition, but we must do everything we can to show her love and remind her how much she means to us.

It is up to us to remember and uphold those vows. We must arise, O compatriots, and answer our mother's call. Remember the promises made to serve her with love, strength, and faith.

Many have laid down their lives for her. These past heroes have labored for our mother, and we ought to ensure that their labor shall never be in vain.

Our mother requires our assistance right now. We should serve her with all our hearts and might—united as her children. She needs our help, and we can only restore her to the caring, loving, and attentive soul she once was if we are united in freedom, peace, and unity.

We must be patient with her and show her the same love and care she has shown us. Our responsibility is to remind her not to give up when her children's lives are at stake. We must address her by name so she will remember how wonderful she is.

Nigeria, our mother, deserves her greatness once more. We must also hold each of her children accountable, including the older ones who lead this large family, and demand that they prioritize our family's well-being.

The older children are almost entirely to blame for our mother's changes. Nigeria used to care deeply. She was gentle with her children and generously provided for their needs. But now that she's turned cold and bitter, please indulge me in a trip down memory lane.

I think of a time when she was willing to be lenient, and we could afford to live in her home. She permitted the prices of things to be low and friendly. And yes, we did moan, groan, and complain that we wished things were cheaper.

But now I would gladly be teleported back to 2016, when a bag of rice was NGN 12,000, rather than the price of 2022 when it was NGN 24,500. We miss what we had and beg for a reprise. The rapid increase in the cost of living has made life unbearable for the children of Nigeria.

Our elders leading this family need to take urgent steps to address this issue and alleviate the suffering of its members. Perhaps a remembrance of what we had and then lost is in order. A comparison of the difference six years can make.

IT IS TIME TO REVIVE THE GOOD OLD DAYS.

A NEW NIGERIA IS POSSIBEE

Basic Necessities	2016	2022
Rice {50 kg}	NGN 12, 000	NGN 24, 500
Tomato {5 pcs}	NGN 125	NGN 300
Beef {1 kg}	NGN 400	NGN 1, 200
Chicken {1 kg}	NGN 1, 000	NGN 2, 200
Turkey {1 kg}	NGN 1, 000	NGN 2, 600
Onion {5 pcs}	NGN 50	NGN 250
Cooking Oil {5 liters}	NGN 1, 700	NGN 5, 600
Yam {1 pc}	NGN 600	NGN 900
Garri {1 bowl}	NGN 350	NGN 1, 000

Mother used to be generous with the amount of beef on my plate of jollof rice, but lately, she can only afford half a boiled egg. My boiled yam was topped with eggs fried with milk, butter, onion, and tomatoes back then, and now I can get by with just a few tablespoons of palm oil.

I wish I could say that the cost of basic necessities is the only thing that has taken a hit, but I'm afraid not. So many things have gone wrong since we stopped respecting, loving, and caring for our mother, Nigeria.

For one thing, exchange rates have plummeted. It is sad to recall that it was **NGN 199** to the dollar in **2016**. Worse, we can no longer determine the actual value of the naira. The naira is fixed at **414** to the dollar on the official market, but on the black market, where many businesses get their supplies, it is worth **NGN 582** as of **2022**.

Our troubles don't stop here, I'm afraid. Despite Nigeria's abundance, our mother suffers from neglect, and her potential for greatness remains squandered.

She is Africa's largest oil producer, but her children frequently encounter scarcity. We have neglected all four of her refineries, and our elders living in Abuja have spent **$7 billion** each year on importing fuel.

LET US PAY TRIBUTE TO OUR MOTHER'S LEGACY BY IMAGINING AND REALIZING NEW, BETTER DREAMS THAT WILL LAST A LIFETIME.

A NEW NIGERIA IS POSSIBEE

The insecurity in this house appears to be worsening as well. We are now dealing with terror groups and armed bandits. The combination of low exports, insecurity, and infrastructure gaps is frightening. Over 14.5 million Nigerian children suffer from food insecurity, with many internally displaced.

Every day, I pray for our broken home. I beseech the God of our creation to guide our noble cause. I pray that He will direct our elders in leading this family and teach our youth the truth.

I beg Him to allow this family to grow in love and honesty. I seek His guidance in assisting all Nigerian children in living just and true lives and attaining great lofty heights.

Our home is a great nation; we must build it so peace and justice can reign.

CHAPTER 3

Failed State Syndrome

Some topics should start with a definition, and a term like ***failed state*** is an example of a subject needing explanation. Because the phrase is subjective and there is no fixed, agreed-upon definition, "failure," like beauty, is in the eye of the beholder.

Nevertheless, a state is labeled "failed" once it can't consistently and legitimately enforce its laws or provide its citizens with essential goods and services. It can lead to a breakdown in social order, increased violence, and a lack of economic growth.

Corruption, political instability, and high levels of poverty are all common indicators of a failed state. Other typical factors contributing to a state's failure include insurgency, high crime rates, an ineffective and impenetrable bureaucracy, as well as, judicial incompetence, and military interference in politics.

It further brings us to the concept of "***failed state syndrome.***" It refers to a country that can no longer provide essential services to its citizens, such as health care, education, infrastructure, and an effective legal system.

Poverty, political factionalism, corruption, civil unrest, terrorism, and a lack of democratic institutions are all problems that failed states face. And these factors contribute to severe economic decline, population displacement, and overall lower living standards.

Failed states may exhibit a variety of indicators that demonstrate their instability, such as a weakened economy, increased levels of crime, a decrease in personal safety, and an inability to control their borders. Failed states can experience political violence, civil war, economic disaster, environmental disruption, and more.

Furthermore, failed states often can't provide fundamental services to their citizens, such as health care, education, and job opportunities. As a result, people living in failed states often experience poverty, hunger, and extreme social alienation.

In many cases, the government in a failed state is so weakened or ineffective in its ability to address the needs of its citizens that international aid and intervention become required in order to restore some level of normalcy and stability.

The "**Three Failed State Syndromes**" refers to the collapse of a state's political, economic, and social institutions. Violence, corruption, and poverty are common characteristics of these syndromes. In such cases, the government fails to provide vital services to its citizens, which leads to a breakdown of law and order.

Failed State: This is not a phrase coined by the author to frighten or shock Nigeria into action. No, the term originated in the 1990s to describe Somalia. A country that descended into chaos after a coup deposed its dictator in 1991, and clans began fighting among themselves.

The absence of a legitimate, functioning government in Somalia facilitated the rise of armed militants and terrorist groups, resulting in years of humanitarian suffering. However, they are not the only country declared a failed state.

RECOGNIZING THE PROBLEM IS THE FIRST STEP TOWARD GENUINE CHANGE.

A NEW NIGERIA IS POSSIBLE

CORRUPTION, WEAK INSTITUTIONS, AND A LACK OF ACCOUNTABILITY ARE ALL ISSUES THAT NEED ADDRESSING.

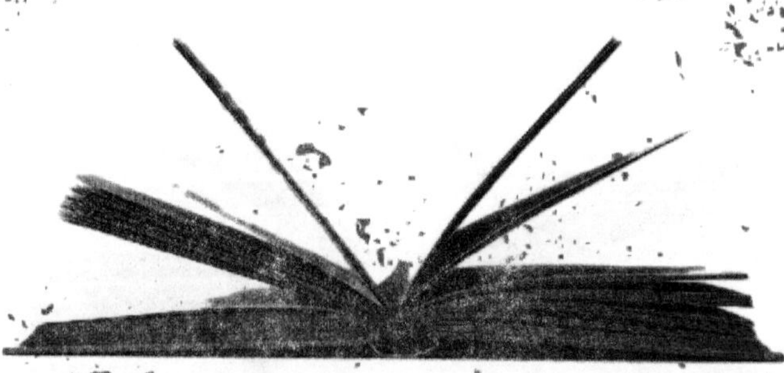

A NEW NIGERIA IS POSSIBEE

Despite being one of the regional giants in the production and supply of crude oil, Syria's civil war has caused the complete breakdown of the country's infrastructure, resulting in the displacement of millions of people, widespread poverty, food insecurity, and violence that has spread far beyond the country's borders.

Yemen, another failed state, has been mired in dispute for years, with limited access to basic necessities like food and clean water and one of the world's highest levels of poverty.

Finally, Afghanistan's government has to grapple with a resurgent Taliban, localized insurgencies, state fragility, and a vulnerable economy. The lack of access to the rule of law, security, and simple services for the majority of Afghans is fueling instability.

So I challenge any Nigerian who picks up this book to consider and honestly answer the following questions: *Are we in a state of fragility or failure? Can we afford to fall even further than we have? Do we want to be ranked alongside Iraq, Haiti, Zimbabwe, Yemen, Somalia, Chad, Sudan, Congo, Afghanistan, Pakistan, Guinea, Syria, and others?*

When you consider Nigeria's current state of stability and prosperity, it's a sobering thought. While the country has not yet reached the levels of conflict and poverty witnessed in the countries listed, there are clear indicators that we are heading in that direction.

The ongoing insurgency in the northeast, the rampant corruption and lack of accountability in government, and the persistent ethnic and religious tensions all contribute to a sense of fragility in the country. It is crucial that we take action to address these issues and prevent Nigeria from slipping further into instability and failure.

One of Nigeria's biggest challenges is the lack of access to necessary services for many of its citizens. Despite being one of the wealthiest countries in Africa, millions of Nigerians still lack access to clean water, electricity, healthcare, and education.

Issues like this undermine the country's economic potential and create a sense of hopelessness and frustration among the population.

Furthermore, the lack of security in many parts of the country has made it difficult for businesses to operate, discouraging investment and hindering economic growth.

Without addressing these underlying issues, Nigeria's future remains uncertain.

A phrase is utilized repeatedly in this chapter to highlight the importance of this subject. I've used the term ***"essential/fundamental/simple/necessary services"*** several times because a country steeped in poverty and instability is a failed state.

In order to improve the lives of its citizens, Nigeria must address the root causes of its economic problems, such as corruption and inadequate infrastructure. Only then can the country hope to become prosperous and stable.

CHAPTER 4

State Capture

Let me tell you about a small kingdom that once existed long ago. The kingdom was situated high in the mountains, surrounded by lush forests. It was a peaceful land with kind people and wise rulers. They valued fairness and justice, and everyone got equal treatment. However, all that changed when a band of mercenaries arrived in the kingdom.

The mercenaries made deals with wealthy landowners, offering protection in exchange for a hefty fee. The landowners were quick to agree and began to amass wealth and power.

You see, the once incorruptible kingdom split into two classes: the wealthy landowners, who had the mercenaries' protection, and the poor farmers, who were left to fend for themselves. The once-existent sense of equality in the kingdom was no more.

Soon, the mercenaries had taken control of the kingdom and its resources. They taxed the people heavily and used the money to further their interests, paying little mind to the citizens. They began rigging elections and appointing their cronies to key positions in the government, creating an atmosphere of corruption and injustice.

The kingdom's people suffered greatly under this rule but were powerless to stop it. They knew speaking out against the mercenaries would result in harsher repercussions. As a result, the ambitions of the corruptible few governed the needs of the many.

After years of poor leadership, a young man from the kingdom decided to take matters into his own hands. He organized a protest against the mercenaries and encouraged other citizens to take a stand with him. After much struggle, the citizens were successful, and the mercenaries expelled from the kingdom.

With the mercenaries gone, the citizens reclaimed their kingdom, restoring justice and fairness. Resolute in their decisions for a better future where justice would always prevail and no one would again be able to seize control through state capture.

To ensure this, the citizens created a solid democratic system to uphold the people's right to participate in their government. Because they lacked a democratic system, they had become susceptible to state capture.

But what happens when a country already has a democratic system in place? What happens to a country that claims to be for the people but appears to be gliding, if not already glided, into the hands of a select few?

Let us ponder these questions while this humble author explains what state capture is and the consequences of having a select few run a country with the goal of lining their pockets and indulging their greed and ambition.

So, what exactly is state capture? State capture refers to the process by which private individuals or organizations gain control over government institutions, policies, and decision-making processes to advance their own interests at the expense of the public good.

It often involves corrupt practices such as bribery, extortion, and nepotism and can have severe consequences for democratic governance, economic development, and social welfare.

In recent years, state capture has become an increasingly prominent issue in many countries, particularly in emerging markets where weak institutions and low levels of transparency make it easier for powerful actors to influence government policies and regulations.

State capture can have disastrous consequences for a country's economy and society. When private interests take control of government decision-making processes, they often prioritize their own profits over the needs of the public.

It can result in policies that benefit a small group of wealthy individuals while harming the bulk of the population. State capture can also erode public trust in government institutions, which can have long-term consequences for a country's political stability and social cohesion.

State capture isn't just about skewing public policy to favor some corporations over others; it's also about strategically weakening that part of the state's law enforcement mechanism that might crack down on corruption.

A SYSTEM FAILS WHEN THE DESIRES OF THE FEW OUTWEIGH THE NEEDS OF THE MAJORITY.

A NEW NIGERIA IS POSSIBLE

For instance, if traditional corruption entails paying a bribe to every police officer who catches you speeding, state capture involves having your car outfitted with police lights so that no officer dares to stop you from driving too fast again. Rather than paying to get away with breaking the law, you pay to make the law work for you.

State capture can happen in any country, regardless of its development level or political system. It is, however, more common in countries with weak institutions, low transparency, and high levels of corruption.

Evidence suggests it is also a problem in developed countries, where governments and businesses have close ties and economic interests are frequently intertwined.

Russia, Ukraine, South Africa, and ***Brazil*** are examples of countries that have experienced state capture. It also exists in other countries across ***Asia, Europe*** and in ***America***. Also in countries where the military, ethnic groups, kleptocratic politicians, or organized criminal groups gain enormous power and shape laws and policies. It is true, for example, in ***Colombia, Pakistan,*** and conflict zones in ***Sub-Saharan Africa.***

WHAT HAPPENS TO A COUNTRY THAT CLAIMS TO BE FOR THE PEOPLE BUT APPEARS TO BE GLIDING, IF NOT ALREADY GLIDED, INTO THE HANDS OF A SELECT FEW?

I get it; reality can be daunting. So, allow me to entertain and relax you with a story about a *"country"* called Rangarstan. Rangarstan was a country plagued by corruption and organized crime, with its citizens frustrated.

The corrupt leadership had led their nation into a downward spiral, and their dreams of prosperity were further away than ever before. They yearned for change, but the political process had become thwarted by the same political elites who had enriched themselves while the rest of the people suffered.

Much of the country's wealth flowed through a tight circle of businessmen and politicians colluding to gain total control of the state. The citizens felt helpless and frustrated as their voices were not getting heard, and corruption was rampant. The government's lack of transparency and accountability only increased their frustration with the system.

By day, the government appeared democratic, but behind the scenes, decisions were reached, and actions were taken by the powerful few, undermining the wishes of the many. Unsurprisingly, criticism of their actions got suppressed, leaving the citizens without a strong voice to bring about any meaningful reform.

Yet, remarkably, one day, the citizens of Rangarstan awoke to find that, overnight, their dream of a better future had become a reality. Without even an incredible display of mass organization and daring, the people had back control of their own destinies.

Even though there hadn't been a single event of great unity, the people had successfully defeated state capture and reclaimed control. This accomplishment demonstrated the power of a dream. They had finally reclaimed their homeland, and the people of Rangarstan could now begin to rebuild.

It was an opportunity to repair the broken political and economic systems that had previously held them back. They rejoiced in their newfound freedom to express their ideas, speak out against injustice, and collaborate in building a stronger, more prosperous future. With the end of state capture, the people of Rangarstan could begin constructing a better future.

Don't you wish it were that simple? You go to bed, envision a better country, and then wake up to find it has become a reality. But, as we all know, a dream can only become a reality through hard work. Without action, a dream is just that—a dream.

Did you think about my question? What are your thoughts? Are we victims of state capture, or is our vehicle on its way there? It makes no difference which answers you give since it would seem that we must nevertheless learn how to address state capture.

Addressing state capture requires reforms and improvements across a whole range of institutions. We need to enhance the accountability of political leaders, regulatory reform, and transparency in political financing.

Furthermore, strengthening the independence of law enforcement and the judiciary is critical to holding those who engage in state capture accountable and bringing them to justice. To effectively address this complex issue, a comprehensive approach is required.

Whatever your position on where this country is currently, we ought to realize how dangerous it is for a few to control the fate of millions of lives.

CHAPTER 5

The Success We Were Denied

1960 is a landmark year in world history because it brought about the independence of numerous countries. Nations such as **Nigeria**, **Benin**, **Togo**, **Cameroon**, **Senegal**, **Zambia**, **Ivory Coast**, **Congo**, **Gabon**, **Somalia**, **Mali**, and other African nations achieved independence.

Also, newly independent countries such as **Indonesia**, **Malta**, **Cyprus**, the **Maldives**, and **Qatar** emerged in the 1960s. These countries embarked on their journey with a strong sense of independence, unity, and civic responsibility.

However, despite the joy and optimism that followed these newfound liberties, several countries

countries faced significant challenges in the subsequent years. Economic instability, political corruption, and social unrest plagued many of these nations, leading to disillusionment among their citizens.

Notwithstanding these setbacks, numerous success stories emerged. In this chapter, we'll look at some of these success stories to see where we, in Nigeria, went wrong. Countries such as **Botswana** and **Mauritius** are examples of success stories, having achieved stable economic growth and good governance despite similar challenges.

This chapter will compare the progress of some of the countries listed above with Nigeria's economic performance by breaking down GDP per capita, inflation rates, and other economic indicators.

WE SHOULDN'T LET PAST FAILURES OR SETBACKS DEFINE OUR FUTURE.

A NEW NIGERIA IS POSSIBEE

NIGERIA: A BRIEF HISTORY

Looking back to the 1960s, Nigeria was ahead of some emerging Asian countries like China, Indonesia, Malaysia, South Korea, and Taiwan.

This country's potential was clear, and its GDP per capita was comparable to that of Indonesia. However, our paths diverged dramatically over the next few decades.

Nigeria's GDP per capita stagnated between 1970 and 2000, while Indonesia's more than quadrupled. Meanwhile, the economies of Malaysia, Singapore, and South Korea have grown by a factor of twenty or more.

Tragically, Nigeria failed to effectively harness its oil wealth, allowing it to slip through its fingers like sand.

Following two decades of independence, a major feature of Nigeria's economy in the 1980s was that we were a net exporter of refined petroleum products, accounting for 87 percent of export receipts and 77 percent of Federal government revenue in 1988.

The exchange rate as of 1980 was a dollar to 0.80 kobo. However, due to mismanagement and corruption in the oil sector, Nigeria's economy has since become heavily reliant on crude oil exports and suffers from a lack of diversification, making it vulnerable to fluctuations in global oil prices. As of 2022, the exchange rate is approximately 1 dollar to 670 naira.

Nigeria currently has a population of **220,762,058** people, making it the most populated country in Africa and the seventh most populated country in the world as of **May 15, 2023**. With an estimated **2.51%** increase by **2025** and nearly doubling our current population by **2050**, we will reach **401,315,000**.

It's evident that in order to achieve long-term stability and growth, Nigeria needs to implement policies that promote economic diversification and reduce its reliance on oil exports. But I'll let our historical data speak for itself.

WHEN NATIONS FAIL TO GRASP TRANSFORMATIVE MOMENTS, THEY FIND THEMSELVES CAUGHT IN A CYCLE OF PERPETUAL RETROGRESSION.

A NEW NIGERIA IS POSSIBEE

Nigeria GDP - Historical Data

YEAR	GDP	PER APITA	GROWTH
2021	$440.83B	$2,066	3.65%
2020	$432.20B	$2,075	-1.79%
2019	$448.12B	$2,204	2.21%
2018	$421.74B	$2,126	1.92%
2017	$375.75B	$1,942	0.81%
2016	$404.65B	$2,145	-1.62%
2015	$493.03B	$2,680	2.65%
2014	$574.18B	$3,201	6.31%
2013	$520.12B	$2,977	6.67%
2012	$463.97B	$2,728	4.23%
2011	$414.47B	$2,505	5.31%
2010	$366.99B	$2,280	8.01%
2009	$295.01B	$1,884	8.04%
2008	$339.48B	$2,228	6.76%
2007	$278.26B	$1,876	6.59%

2006	$238.45B	$1,652	6.06%
2005	$175.67B	$1,250	6.44%
2004	$135.76B	$993	9.25%
2003	$104.74B	$787	7.35%
2002	$95.05B	$734	15.33%
2001	$72.80B	$577	5.92%
2000	$69.45B	$565	5.02%
1999	$59.37B	$496	0.58%
1998	$54.60B	$468	2.58%
1997	$54.46B	$479	2.94%
1996	$51.08B	$460	4.20%
1995	$44.06B	$407	-0.07%
1994	$33.83B	$321	-1.81%
1993	$27.75B	$270	-2.04%
1992	$47.79B	$477	4.63%
1991	$49.12B	$503	0.36%

1990	$54.04B	$568	11.78%
1989	$44.00B	$474	1.92%
1988	$49.65B	$550	7.33%
1987	$52.68B	$598	3.20%
1986	$54.81B	$639	0.06%
1985	$73.75B	$882	5.91%
1984	$73.48B	$903	-1.12%
1983	$97.09B	$1,224	-10.92%
1982	$142.77B	$1,845	-6.80%
1981	$164.48B	$2,188	-13.13%
1980	$64.20B	$880	4.20%
1979	$47.26B	$668	6.76%
1978	$36.53B	$532	-5.76%
1977	$36.04B	$541	6.02%
1976	$36.31B	$562	9.04%
1975	$27.78B	$442	-5.23%

1974	$24.85B	$406	11.16%
1973	$15.16B	$254	5.39%
1972	$12.27B	$211	3.36%
1971	$9.18B	$162	14.24%
1970	$12.55B	$226	25.01%
1969	$6.63B	$122	24.20%
1968	$5.20B	$98	-1.25%
1967	$5.20B	$100	-15.74%
1966	$6.37B	$125	-4.25%
1965	$5.87B	$118	4.89%
1964	$5.55B	$114	4.95%
1963	$5.17B	$108	8.58%
1962	$4.91B	$105	4.10%
1961	$4.47B	$97	0.19%
1960	$4.20B	$93	%

While we can't look at 60 years of GDP for every country, we can look at what they did differently or, more accurately, what we did wrong. Nigeria is a great nation, but we have fallen behind in many areas.

Please take note of every detail in the countries listed, as what these countries have done should serve as our blueprint—a map of the roads to take and the path to walk on.

We must learn from their successes and tailor their strategies to our circumstances. Only then can we hope to catch up with the rest of the world and fulfill our true national potential.

Cameroon: a brief history

Since gaining its independence from France in 1960, Cameroon has enjoyed relative stability, allowing for the development of roads and railways as well as profitable agricultural and petroleum industries.

Cameroon has become one of the most prosperous African states, with the largest economy in the **Central African Economic and Monetary Community (CEMAC)**.

To protect its economy from recession and maintain confidence in its currency, the Central African CFA franc, Cameroon employs strict fiscal adjustment measures.

The country's GDP for 2021 was **$45.34 billion**, an **11.2% increase** from 2020, with the economy largely dependent on its exports of natural resources, including petroleum, minerals, timber, and agricultural products such as coffee, cotton, cocoa, maize, and cassava.

The projection of Cameroon's current population of about **26.55 million** is **50 million** by **2050** and then **89.62 million** by **2099**. Despite negative net migration, Cameroon's population is growing at a 2.59% annual rate, adding over 600,000 people.

Botswana: a brief history

Botswana is a small, landlocked country in Southern Africa with just over two million citizens and a long history of strong financial growth.

Since independence in 1966, Botswana has achieved remarkable economic success, becoming one of Sub-Saharan Africa's fastest-growing economies.

Its GDP per capita rose from just **US$134** in 1966 to nearly **US$6,800** in 2017. This impressive growth has been attributed primarily to Botswana's unequaled commitment to development of human resources, prudent fiscal management, and sensible investment practices.

Among the most notable factors contributing to Botswana's economic success have been decades of firm financial discipline, high levels of public spending financing infrastructure and social security, and an effective fight against corruption. The country has achieved remarkable success in democratic governance and public health.

These successes have aided in the country's extensive integration with the rest of the world economy, as evidenced by its exceptionally high portion of foreign direct investment as a percent of GDP.

In addition, Botswana's favorable economic environment has been a boon to the industry, particularly the diamond mining sector. This industry's dominance has made Botswana a crucial player in the international diamond trade, accounting for nearly 70% of the world's diamond production.

This dynamic has helped fuel one of the world's highest rates of economic growth over the past two decades, with the economy expected to continue expanding over the next ten years.

Maldives: a brief history

Maldives is a small South Asian island nation located in the Indian Ocean. Their current population is **567,778** as of May 15, 2023. Despite its small size, the country is one of the fastest-growing economies in the world, boasting the highest Gross Domestic Product in South Asia.

The economy has experienced substantial growth since 1991, when the country held its first democratic elections, resulting in a stable political environment and significant economic reforms. The reform policies of the post-1991 period have provided an ideal environment for the creation of a prosperous and diversified market economy.

Maldives' first-ever Economic Reform Program, implemented in 1995, focused on identifying and executing liberalization policies that promote foreign investment in key sectors, diversification of economic activities, opening up the domestic market, and adopting sound economic regulations.

Devastating natural disasters, such as the 2004 tsunami, have disrupted the country's economic growth on several occasions; however, the Maldives remains one of the fastest-growing economies in the world.

The country's economy saw a 10 percent growth over the past few decades, with a projection to continue to grow steadily in the years to come. The government of Maldives has identified tourism as the main engine of economic growth and catalyzed its development as the number one foreign currency earner, making up approximately **28.7%** of GDP in 2021.

The growth and expansion of the tourism sector have been supported by the government's wider efforts to modernize the country.

With recent projects such as the development of larger airports and harbors, improvement of transport and civil aviation infrastructure, the establishment of educational institutions and healthcare facilities, and improvements to electricity and water networks.

The government also supports initiatives to increase agricultural yield, including grant support to farmers as well as technology transfers to increase crop productivity. With a high reliance on imported food items (which make up nearly 80% of the food supply), the country's food security depends heavily on external factors such as imports, so developing a secure and sustainable local food supply remains a priority.

Overall, the government of Maldives is determined to accelerate the economic growth and improvements of the country's economic indicators by adopting policies and strategies that ensure sustainable economic growth and development in the medium and long term.

China: a brief history

The economy of China has seen historically strong growth over the past several decades, contributing to the nation's global economic prominence. It began to reform its state-owned economy in 1979 in an effort to open its markets and promote the growth of private enterprise.

This undertaking has led to an unprecedented period of sustained economic growth that transformed China from a poverty-stricken nation to the world's second-largest economy, behind only the United States.

In 1980, China's GDP estimation was around **$214 billion** in current US dollars. By 2018, it had skyrocketed to more than **$13 trillion**, constituting more than 17% of the world's total economic output.

Additionally, China's population is currently 1,455,204,598 billion, making it the world's most populous country.

Its economy has experienced rapid structural changes since the launch of its economic reforms. The process of industrialization and urbanization accelerated in the 1990s and 2000s as Chinese citizens flocked to cities in large numbers. Household incomes have also risen significantly over recent years, as wages have generally kept up with economic growth.

It has enabled the Chinese middle class to emerge, resulting in faster growth in China's consumer markets.

China's ascension to its first-ever ranking as the world's second-largest economy is a result of both the economic reforms of the past four decades and the nation's significant population size, which has allowed it to benefit from economies of scale. As the country pursues higher levels of economic growth and expansion, it will be critical to keep these structural dynamics in mind to preserve the potential for future development.

Qatar: a brief history

With a current population of **3,020,219**, Qatar is a small peninsula located on the Persian Gulf and is considered one of the fastest developing countries in the world. It has seen exponential growth since its inception as an independent state in 1971.

Qatar has become an affluent nation, focusing on modernizing infrastructure and driving economic innovation. It has become a sought-after destination for international businesses and investments. The GDP has grown significantly over the last two decades because of its relatively diverse economy, with a cursor on the oil and gas sector.

Though the oil sector continues to be the biggest contributor to Qatar's economy, accounting for more than 80% of GDP in 2018, the country is actively diversifying its economy by developing non-oil and tertiary industries.

Qatar's economy grew rapidly in the 2000s, owing primarily to high energy prices and significant capital investments; however, during the global financial crisis in 2009 and 2015, Qatar's economy suffered because of a slowdown in oil prices.

Per capita income has also grown significantly over the years, with Qatar now boasting one of the highest per capita incomes in the world. As a result of oil wealth and investment to achieve social and economic development, Qatar has experienced rapid economic growth over the past decade, leading to increased living standards.

As part of Qatar's economic vision and reforms, the country has undertaken a series of economic and fiscal policies aimed at diversifying its income sources, increasing competitiveness, and setting Qatar up for sustainable economic growth in the future.

India: a brief history

India is known as a significant player in the global economy. With a population of nearly **1.4 billion** and a large base of potential consumers, the country has typically maintained a healthy Gross Domestic Product (GDP) growth rate.

After gaining independence in 1947, the Indian government introduced a series of Five-Year Plans to stimulate the economy.

These plans introduced regulations and investments to provide the foundation for economic development and, in the process, triggered India's impressive economic growth.

In the 1980s, India shifted from a closed, highly regulated economy to a more open one with relatively few controls on distribution, pricing, and foreign trade and investments. This switch, known as economic liberalization, improved prospects for long-term growth and capital inflows from abroad.

The 1990s also saw India's poverty levels decline due to increasing economic growth, while the agricultural sector saw transformative change due to the introduction of modern farming technologies.

India implemented the Goods and Services Tax (GST) in July 2017 to create a unified tax system across all of the country's states. The move has provoked both positive and negative reactions, and its impact on the economic dynamics remains uncertain. India is also looking for ways to reduce its reliance on agriculture as a key sector of its economy.

Despite the uncertainty, India's GDP and economic stability suggest that the country will continue to be an important player in the global economy for years to come.

Singapore: a brief history

Singapore has one of the most successful economies in the world, with a nominal GDP per capita of **$52,927** in 2018, ranking it as the second-highest in Asia and the third-highest globally.

The country implemented measures to liberalize the economy and attract more foreign investment after gaining independence in 1965.

Low taxes, liberal banking policies, and investments in physical infrastructure were all part of this strategy. Which resulted in rapid growth in the manufacturing and services sectors, and Singapore's economy skyrocketed.

Technology and innovation helped push growth further, while free trade agreements with other countries, such as the US and China, further boosted the economically diverse nation.

Singapore is now a major business and financial hub in Asia, with a world-class infrastructure, a highly skilled and educated workforce, and open and business-friendly policies.

The Singaporean economy is highly resilient and has been able to adapt to global economic changes, such as the financial crisis of 2007–2008 and the

European debt crisis of 2011–2012.

The current population of Singapore in 2023 is **6,014,723**, and with the economy being among the fastest-growing in the world, Singapore has continued to remain competitive in the world market and attract more foreign investment.

***

This author could go on and on about these countries, and I know it's easy to dismiss them because most of them are small and thus manageable, but consider China's progress in just 30 years.

We have not accomplished a quarter of what they have in twice as many years since our inception. I'm not the best mathematician, but according to my calculations, China has more than six times our population.

Nigeria must improve if it is to catch up with China and other rapidly developing countries. And this entails investing in education, infrastructure, and technology to create a more competitive economy and raise our citizens' standard of living.

It isn't a job for the government alone; it requires collaborative efforts between the public and private sectors. Encouragement of entrepreneurship and innovation, along with the promotion of foreign investment, can also contribute to economic growth and creation of more job opportunities for our growing population.

Furthermore, Nigeria must address its challenges with corruption and political instability, which have hindered progress in the past.

I will state this again: the government must prioritize transparency and accountability to build trust and confidence among the public.

Nigeria has immense potential, but we, as a nation, must take bold and decisive action to realize it. By focusing on these key areas, Nigeria can become a major player in the global economy and improve the lives of its citizens.

Chapter 6

A Nightmare or A Dream

The year is 2050, and the world we once knew is gone. In its stead is a land of total ruin, starvation, poverty, diseases, and death. The air is thick with pollution, and the oceans, filled with waste.

The sun was scorching hot against the parched ground, and the sky was an oppressively barren orange with the faintest hint of a distant desert storm. In the distance stood a line of dust-covered figures coming closer, barely discernible due to the dust storm surrounding them. As they come closer, the figures take on definition, and an uneasiness fills the air as it becomes clear they are soldiers.

Our hero in this story, a young man named Abeba,

took cover. He was used to the demands these men made in the name of the president whenever they visited their district, but this time something felt different.

As he watched them approach, he couldn't shake the feeling that this visit would be unlike any other. Abeba's heart raced as the soldiers drew nearer, their expressions stern and unyielding.

The new order of things in this world was becoming increasingly oppressive. One could flee, but every turn brought the same sense of foreboding and fear. There was destruction everywhere you looked, no trace of the towns and cities that had once stood proud in the landscape.

On days like these, Abeba remembered the words from a book he had taken to memory. The book foresaw this world and the future that is now his reality—a world where humanity had pushed the limits of nature and paid the price for it.

Abeba wondered if the human race had any hope left or was the human race doomed to live forever in a desolate wasteland. He couldn't help but feel despair wash over him as he gazed out at the barren horizon.

When the soldiers reached his district, everyone stood in a queue, their houses searched, and everything of value, which for most was a loaf of stale bread, was seized and claimed for the president of the land.

Abeba overheard two soldiers speak of a prosperous location far across the sea. The lands and people there were unaffected by the suffering that had befallen them, but the journey was difficult and arduous, with little hope of survival.

After the soldiers had beaten, maimed, and taken all they could, they left for another district, leaving Abeba to look for his friend Kena. He wanted to seek out this new land with his friend, but when he met Kena, he couldn't persuade him.

Kena was a coward, too afraid of change. Though Abeba told him that this new land heeded the warning and implemented the **17 Sustainable Development Goals,** Kena decided to remain in his comfort zone and not take risks.

Although Abeba was disappointed, he respected Kena's decision and embarked on his journey alone. He encountered challenges and obstacles, but his determination to find this new land kept him going.

But left behind, Kena suffered. Because the president had not implemented the 17 goals, their land was now a harsh, unforgiving place. Poverty and starvation had become epidemics; children orphaned on the streets with no one to care for them. Communities struggled to find new food sources as the environment and climate change caused crops to fail. The air was thick with pollution, and the water was now undrinkable.

There was no hope and nothing to look forward to. Every one of the goals had a huge red cross mark on it, indicating failure. The community was on the brink of collapse, with people becoming increasingly desperate for solutions to their problems.

No poverty was one of the goals, but it wasn't the case for Kena and the people of that district. They were struggling to make ends meet, with many families unable to afford basic necessities like food and shelter. Parents abandoned their children on the street because they had no means to provide for them.

They only knew hunger instead of ***zero hunger.*** There was no ***good health and well-being***, only sickness and death. It was near impossible to get a ***quality education*** when the ones who could read were slowly dying and giving way to illiterates all over the district.

And although the fifth goal was ***gender equality***, the men of Kena District, with no real power, picked on the women and reduced them to second-class citizens. ***Clean water and sanitation*** became myths as water shortages became more rampant.

Instead of ***affordable and clean energy***, electricity became a thing of the past. Over 400 million people in all the districts under the president's rule, and 90% grew up without electricity.

Every other goal on the list was left undone. From ***decent Work and Economic Growth to Industry, Innovation, and Infrastructure, Reduced Inequality, and Sustainable Cities and Communities.***

Others that they failed to achieve were ***Responsible Consumption and Production, Climate Action, Life Below Water, Life on Land, Peace, and Justice Strong institutions, and lastly, partnerships to achieve the goal.***

Kena was a resident of a failed community.

It was reminiscent of a post-apocalyptic landscape, with much of the world reduced to ashes and rubble. The community's environment and resources got harmed by a lack of responsible consumption and production, as well as a lack of climate action.

But while Kena was content to stay in that state, afraid of change, Abeba was not. After a treacherous journey, he found the country across the ocean. It was a country he could only describe as paradise. The country's leaders took the warning to heart and achieved everything listed in the 17 goals.

This country was called Daltania, and there were others like it. The leaders of Daltania saw fit to make a change rather than relying solely on their traditional methods of governance and development.

With the ambition and vision to become a prosperous country, they decided to enact the Sustainable Development Goals (SDGs), a set of 17 global objectives to end poverty, protect the planet, and ensure prosperity for all.

The leaders of Daltania knew that they would need to be committed to this mission if they were to succeed. They created a plan to reduce poverty, create more jobs, improve health care, and promote education.

They also worked to protect their environment by establishing protected areas, implementing renewable energy sources, and reducing pollution.

Through hard work and dedication, Daltania achieved the SDGs and became a thriving and prosperous nation.

THE FUTURE MAY SEEM BLEAK, BUT WE MUST MAKE IT A DREAM RATHER THAN A NIGHTMARE.

A NEW NIGERIA IS POSSIBEE

Let us leave the world of fiction for a moment and think of our future as Nigerians. We must strive to achieve the 17 Sustainable Development Goals set by the United Nations, as they provide a blueprint for a better and more sustainable future for all.

Nigeria is the largest economy in Africa and a leading nation on the continent. As a result, it is critical that we ensure it is not only economically prosperous but also socially and environmentally sustainable.

The Sustainable Development Goals (SDGs) of the United Nations are a set of goals adopted by world leaders in 2015 to guide global development efforts over the next 15 years. These goals aim to end poverty, protect the environment, and ensure that we live in peace and prosperity.

The SDGs are particularly relevant to Nigeria, as this country faces many challenges related to poverty, inequality, and poor environmental conditions.

In order to achieve the SDGs, we must address these challenges head-on and implement policies and programs that will promote sustainable development.

First and foremost, Nigeria must address poverty. We have the world's highest rate of extreme poverty, with over 80 million people living on less than $1.90 a day. To achieve the SDGs, Nigeria must invest in poverty alleviation programs and policies that help reduce poverty levels and promote economic growth. It could include programs such as job creation, access to credit, and social protection.

Second, Nigeria needs to reduce inequality. The country has a large number of people living in extreme poverty but also a large number of extremely wealthy people.

This inequality negatively impacts the country's development because it perpetuates poverty and stifles economic growth. Investment in programs that promote social inclusion, equal access to resources, and initiatives that reduce wealth disparities is required to reduce this inequality.

Third, we must tackle environmental issues. Our country deals with several environmental issues, from deforestation to air pollution to water scarcity.

To achieve the SDGs, Nigeria must invest in programs that promote environmental sustainability and reduce the country's ecological footprint. We could include initiatives such as renewable energy, improved waste management, and the protection of natural resources.

Achieving the SDGs is a critical goal for Nigeria. By tackling poverty, reducing inequality, and protecting the environment, the country can ensure that it is both economically prosperous and socially and environmentally sustainable.

Only then can we truly become a leader in Africa and the world.

It is up to us to choose what we make of Nigeria. Whether it is to be a nightmare, one we cannot escape, or a dream we never want to awaken.

Chapter 7

Nigeria: A Story of Hope

A country is the collective aspiration of its people—their hopes, dreams, struggles, faith, and desire for a better tomorrow to leave to future generations. Every Nigerian determines how the rest of the world perceives this country.

We are all telling the story of Nigeria: of our economy when we sigh at high prices at the local shop; of our healthcare when we complain about government officials embarking on medical tourism abroad; of our education when university students spend months at home because their lecturers are on strike; of our values when people steal public funds, and so on.

And these stories can have a happier ending if we choose to do the right thing wherever we are, no matter how insignificant the action appears. It could be as simple as picking up litter on the street. Every little positive action counts towards creating a better society for ourselves and future generations. Let us all strive to be the change we want to see in the world.

It is often said, rightly by notable novelist **Chinua Achebe**, that Nigeria's 'trouble' is leadership. Good leadership cannot exist without the support of responsible followers. That is how constructive criticism can flourish and how democracy can overcome sycophancy. It's the way hope is built—by casting it into the hearts and minds of people.

Nigeria has always struck me as a great poem yet to be completed. It's a poem that tells the story of our struggle, faith, pain, failures, dreams, and, most importantly, hope. And hope has certainly kept us going as a nation, despite our difficulties.

Nevertheless, we must believe that a better Nigeria will emerge from our dreams because it does not belong to the night or day as we sleep. It belongs to reality—our reality. Everyone must rise up and contribute to the building of our future.

We must sing it. We must dance to it. We must hold it as high as the sun. We must commit it to memory. We must begin writing the poem of this great nation not as placeholders but as stakeholders.

If we are to take our place as constructors, it is time to pick up the pen and start writing. We must capture the essence of our country, its people, and its values in every word we write. Only then can we inspire others to join us in building a brighter future for all.

But for the poem to be true, our words must carry our yearnings for Nigeria beyond the ears of faith and onto the wings of hope. And every generation of us must hold progress in keep for the next to make its run.

So, I shall begin writing our poem of hope and say a prayer for it to carry on from the chief to the infants in the most remote village in Nigeria. May our hope be a beacon of light in the darkest of times, and may it unite us in creating a better world for ourselves and future generations.

Nigeria: A Story of Hope
Of pain and how we learned to cope
The day we flew the flag, the first of its hoists, hope was reborn.
In the hearts of everyone who stood on the grounds of the new nation,
hope shone its light through the darkness of colonialism.
There was nothing left but hope.

The world watched us grow, bearing the burden of nationhood
and casting away the forceful weight of amalgamation.
On the day of independence, it was our will to stay,
to live together on this 923,768 km2 land mass.
To dwell on 853 km of coastline and 34 hectares of arable land
blessed with abundant human and natural resources.

Hosting one of the most diverse ecosystems in the world
with plains, deserts, swamps, mountains, and jungles.
This nation greeted us with over 22,000 animal species
and three distinct climatic zones.
It was our decision to live together,
to travel the hallowed grounds of freedom holding hands.

The scream of "Araba" faded behind our footprints.
We did not write this will in "*British*" or say it in "*American.*"
We sang it in the voices of our people:
the Ibibio, Kanuri, Fulfulde, Tiv, Igala, Hausa, Birom, Zambara,
Ijaw, Kalabari, Igbo, Galambi, Gokana, Idoma, Yoruba,
and the over 520 languages to which we owe our nationhood.

When we left Tafawa Balewa Square that day,
we took the anthem in our hearts, the pledge in our bones,
the flag in our hands and hope in our blood.
Pa Benedict Odiase and Pa Taiwo Akinkunmi
glowing in their gifts to the nation.
But darkness came upon our journey, and the demons came, held our feet,
and dragged us to the ground to scare the will from our hearts.

1966 was a bloody year!
The best of us brought the worst upon us.
We drank and ate our blood and flesh as we broke our oath.
Two nights, did we lose our heads.
Two nights did we suffer.
Two nights in 1966.

They still talk about it in the library in low tones.
If you think 1966 was disastrous, then wait till you see 1967.
It is a story we do not tell at night.
For the children will convulse and die.
We tell it during the day,
when the elements have all washed their feet in clay.

We tell it with a bottle of 'tufiaakwaa' in one hand,
for our mouths must not retain what our stomachs regurgitate.
But how can you see what is invisible; if you haven't been blind?
How can you tell the visions of a madman if you haven't held madness in your trance?
We descended into the belly of the darkness so we might see the light.
Wonder how we weren't consumed by this eclipse of humanity, right?

Here is how we remembered how to hope,
and this is where we learned to cope.
Let us tell the story of Herbert Macaulay,
an excellent Nigerian dubbed the father of Nigeria's Nationalism.
Of how he held hope in his blood as he walked these lands,
nailing firsts on the canvas of history.

Let the world know about his establishment of the NNDP in 1923.
Tell the people how he sparked a pan-Nigerian movement
and inspired the struggle for independence.
Tell them that, before 1923, our mothers marched in Aba in 1920
in the famous Aba Women Riot against the Warrant Chiefs' demand for taxes.
Do not ever stop writing about our greatness.

Tell them how, by 1944, Madam Olufemi Ransome-
Kuti led the Abeokuta Club,
demanding the abolition of flat rate taxes and
inclusion of women
in the local administration from the British
government and the Alake.
They must know that she would go on to inspire
other women.
Women like Madam Adunni Oluwole,
who founded the first woman-led political party in
Nigeria in 1953.

When they think you have said enough,
go on and say some more.
Inform them that Dr. Nnamdi Azikiwe
did not give up.
Nor did Chief Obafemi Awolowo.
What about Sir Ahmadu Bello?
Let us tell their stories.

Tell them the spirit of hope did not die with our
mothers who marched.
They ought to know it was alive and well in 2020
when we banned together and fought against
oppression
Tell them that we stared down the barrel of a gun
and fought for what we believed in.
Tell them that the bodies of our loved ones got stolen
from us.
Tell them that the **#ENDSARS** movement was not
the end of hope.

Tell these stories to your children when the moon is
out on a stroll.
Tell them how we walked out of the darkness of 1966.
Tell them the demons came, held our feet,
and dragged us to the ground to scare the will from
our hearts.
But be careful not to tell them about 1967,
for they may convulse in their sleep and die.

Wait for the sun with a bottle of 'tufiaakwaa,'
for the tale will pour ulcers on your lining.
May God forbid another 1967!
Tell them about the four republics and how we
survived.
Mention the stutters of 1975, 1983, 1985, and 1993.
Show them the tombstone of tyranny.

Let them lift the locks at the gates,
even if it weighs their hands down.
It is, too, their burden to bear.
Take them away while the sun is still awake.
The world must make progress here.
The future is not a destination behind our footprints.

Again, the darkness gathers, and the demons are coming,
crawling on insurgency, banditry, kidnapping, and ritual killings.
But hope does not wait to be born.
It becomes what the heart sees.
With our will intact, we are united.
For together, we stood on the sands of the new nation and forged the will to stay.

We have danced, sang, fought, and died together.
We have seen the darkness vanish in the light.
We know there is hope.
We have hope.
We must keep hope in our blood.
We are hope.

So don't stop telling our stories,
and don't stop writing our poems.
Tell them! Tell them! Tell them!
Tell them how we learned to cope.
Tell them! Tell them! Tell them!
For a new Nigeria is the story of hope.

CHAPTER 8

I Am Nigerian

My name is Dr. Moses Paul, and I'm a Nigerian. And being a Nigerian has a great deal of meaning to me. It means that I come from a country with a rich and deep history, a country that is home to many diverse cultures, languages, religions, and customs.

Being a Nigerian is being part of a community known for its resilience, creativity, and resourcefulness in the face of adversity. And adversity is not unknown to the citizens of this country.

As a Nigerian, I have grown up with a strong sense of community and family and have learned to value the importance of relationships and social connections.

I am proud to be part of a nation that has produced some of the world's most talented artists, musicians, writers, and athletes.

However, as a Nigerian, I'm conscious of our difficulties. We are still dealing with political instability, corruption, poverty, and insecurity. But being a Nigerian also mean that I stand for justice, human rights, and freedom.

I recognize the importance of the Nigerian spirit and perseverance, the resiliency and strength of the Nigerian people, and the uniqueness of the Nigerian culture. I take pride in being a Nigerian and am committed to making our country a better home for all Nigerians.

We at ***The Free Nigerian Movement*** remain committed to mobilizing young Nigerians for the common good and the restoration of democratic ethos. Our allegiance will remain to Nigeria, and our commitment to the promotion of good governance is unshaken.

We are your brothers, sisters, friends, and comrades. We are the embodiment of hope. We are the dream begging to see the light of day. We are Nigerians.

ALL MEN DREAM BUT NOT EQUALLY. THOSE WHO DREAM BY NIGHT IN THE DUSTY RECESSES OF THEIR MINDS WAKE IN THE DAY TO FIND THAT IT WAS VANITY; BUT THE DREAM OF THE DAY ARE DANGEROUS MEN, FOR THEY MIGHT ACT THEIR DREAMS WITH OPEN EYES TO MAKE IMPOSSIBLE.

–Thomas Edward Lawrence

A SOCIETY WHICH DEBASES THE POWER OF IDEAS WHILE EXALTING THE IDEA OF POWER IS NOT ONLY SHORT-SIGHTED BUT FOOLISH IN THE EXTREME.

– Adebayo Adedeji

THERE IS A MYSTERIOUS CYCLE IN HUMAN EVENTS. TO SOME GENERATIONS MUCH IS GIVEN OF OTHERS MUCH IS EXPECTED.

– Franklin Delano Roosevelt